Grandma's Last Lesson

by Tammy Kohnen

illustrated by Alexandra D. Pierce

Grandma's Last Lesson

ISBN 978-1-64458-030-1 (paperback)
ISBN 978-1-64458-031-8 (digital)

Christian Faith Publishing, Inc.
832 Park Avenue
Meadville, PA 16335
www.christianfaithpublishing.com

Printed in the United States of America

Liz rushed around her room, putting things into her suitcase. Her mom asked her to get packed to leave in an hour for her grandparents' house in Minnesota. Her family had made the trip from Iowa several times in the last year, so seven-year-old Liz knew what she needed.

Dad announced everything was set to go. Mom buckled in Liz's five-year-old sister Kate and three-year-old Shelley. Liz thought about her grandma on the long drive. She loved her grandma's cooking and all the attention she gave them. Now she wondered what special gift her grandma had in store for her.

"We're here," Liz announced loudly. She hurried out of her seat belt and skipped into the house.

When she walked through the door, her smile quickly turned to a frown. Something about the kitchen looked wrong. There wasn't the usual smell of a roast cooking in the oven or freshly baked cookies.

"Grandpa, why didn't Grandma bake chocolate chip cookies?" Liz asked.

"Sorry, Liz," Grandpa apologized. "Grandma had to go into the hospital last night. She's been feeling very sick."

The girls looked to their parents with questioning expressions.

"We have something important to tell you. It may make you sad," her mother said.

"Grandma is sick, and the doctors don't have any medicine that can make her well again," her father explained.

"But why, Daddy? Why can't they find a medicine?" Liz asked.

"They just can't, sweetie. They tried every medicine there is, but there just isn't anything to cure the cancer," Mom said while gathering them all into her arms.

"What is cancer again?" Liz asked.

Though she had asked this question a million times since her grandma first got sick last year, she wanted to ask it again, just to be sure. Before they could reply, Grandpa answered.

"Cancer is a sickness people sometimes get. It happens when bad cells kill the good cells in a person's body. But people don't get sick by being with cancer patients. Some people get well again, and some don't," Grandpa said.

11

"I thought Grandma had medicine to make her better?" Liz asked.

"Yes, Liz. Grandma did have medicine at the hospital when the doctors found the cancer last year. But sometimes medicine just can't fight off certain cancer cells," Dad said.

Liz hugged her dad tightly and watched as Shelley crawled up into her mom's lap. She looked up and motioned for Kate to join their bear hug so she wouldn't feel left out. Having everyone close made Liz feel a little better, though it didn't take away the pain Liz felt inside.

"Girls, we're all going to get through this together. Why don't we go see Grandma now?" Dad suggested.

Everyone jumped back in the car for the short ride to the hospital. Liz felt nervous and scared to see Grandma. She remembered when they visited Grandma after she had taken the strong medicine. She looked tired. Her hair had started to fall out, and she was wearing a wig. She hadn't been playing with them as much as she used to.

Liz walked through the hospital doors and brightened when she spotted a flower shop. "Daddy, can we get flowers for Grandma?"

"That's a great idea, Liz. Come on, girls, we'll all pick some out," her dad said.

"Yeah!" they shouted as they skipped down the shiny hallway.

After several minutes deciding which bouquet was the prettiest, they chose a bunch of pink tulips and white mums.

"Grandma's favorite flowers," Dad had said.

"Hi, Grandma," the girls said, entering the hospital room.

Liz looked around the room at all the white things—curtains, bedsheets, a bathrobe, and towels. The room smelled funny, like medicine and cleaning stuff. She decided she would not like staying in a hospital.

Grandma immediately perked up as they all found places to sit.

"How are my three favorite girls?" Grandma asked.

19

"Why are you sick?" Liz blurted out. She couldn't hold the question inside any longer.

"Well, there's something wrong in my stomach, but the doctors are going to make it better. Don't you worry about it, sweetie pie," Grandma quickly answered.

Liz saw her mom and dad look at each other, and she felt confused. Though Grandma was smiling, she wondered why they all looked so sad.

I'll ask them later, she thought.

The second they got into the car Liz burst out, "Mom, is Grandma really going to be okay?"

Mom turned around and replied. "Grandma would like to believe that, and so would we. But this time the doctors can't fix the cancer. Grandma isn't going to get well. She is going to stay at home and a hospice nurse will help us make her comfortable."

"Then why did Grandma say not to worry?" Kate asked.

"It's easier to believe that the doctors can make her well again. Sometimes miracles do happen, and a person does get well. But a lot of times there's not a medicine or prayer that can heal people on earth," Dad replied.

"Can't hospice make Grandma better?" Liz pleaded.

"No, honey. Hospice care means people who can't get well will be cared for in their own home or a care facility. Nurses and volunteers help them through the final days of their life. Hospice also helps families prepare for their loved one's death," Mom explained.

Liz was scared. They had talked a lot about Grandma being sick, but no one had said the word death before. She knew about death, about how you go to sleep and never wake up, and then you go to heaven. She wasn't ready for Grandma to die.

Liz thought about what her mom said and knew she had to do something special for her grandma. By the time Grandma came home from the hospital, the girls had decorated her bedroom with colorful pictures on every wall.

"Wow!" her grandma said when she finally came home and walked into her room. "Let's take a ride on my bed, girls."

The three little girls hopped onto Grandma's new hospital bed with her, and she let them push all the buttons. It was like being on a roller coaster ride.

Grandma stayed in bed most of the time. Sometimes she knew her family, and sometimes she didn't. But every day Mom and Liz read Grandma's favorite book to her, the Bible. Liz felt warm inside when she read to her knowing she was helping. Shelley and Kate wanted to help too and read their storybooks aloud to Grandma.

One day, her parents gathered the girls around them as Grandpa sat quietly in his chair.

"Girls, soon Jesus is going to take Grandma up to heaven with Him," her dad stated.

"Will she be happy there, Daddy?" Liz asked.

"Oh yes! Grandma will love heaven. She will get to see her sister and parents again. She will be very happy there," he said.

"In heaven Grandma will also be well again. She won't have to take any medicine, and she won't have any more pain," Mom quickly added.

"Grandma will be happy to see Jesus!" Shelley chimed in.

"Yes, she will," their dad added.

"But I will miss Grandma," Liz said.

"We all will, Liz. It's never easy letting go of someone you love so much. But we have to trust that God knows what is best," Mom assured her.

Throughout the next few days, her grandma slept more and more. A few days later, during the middle of the night, her grandma's long battle with cancer was over.

Grandpa called hospice, and they came to take care of Grandma before the children awoke. A special car called a hearse came and took Liz's grandma to the funeral home where they would get the body ready for the memorial service.

When Liz awoke, she ran to Grandma's room and saw the empty bed.

"Mom, it's not fair!" she cried. "I wasn't ready yet."

Mom and Dad went to her and pulled her into their arms, hugging her tightly.

"Neither were we, honey, but Grandma was ready to go. She's at peace now," Mom said softly.

Shelley soon appeared at the top of the stairs and saw everyone crying.

"Grandma is with Jesus now. She's happy," Shelley said.

Dad walked over to her and scooped her up into his arms.

"You are so right, Shelley. Grandma is happy. We are only crying because we're going to miss her," Dad said through his tears.

"Me too, Daddy," Shelley agreed.

Then Kate came into the room, saw everyone hugging, and padded over to Grandpa. She crawled into his lap and snuggled up close.

39

Things would not be the same without Grandma. But somehow they all knew they would be okay. They all had each other for comfort, support, and love. God had gotten them all this far, and He would be there to see them through the grieving process as well. Liz knew that God had given children grandmothers to show them what love was all about.

About the Author

Tammy Kohnen is a native Minnesotan and mother of three girls. She has been married to her high school sweetheart for thirty years. She has had various careers over the years, but "author" may be her favorite one. After being her mother-in-law's caregiver throughout her battle with breast cancer, she wanted to help other families walk through this journey. It is her hope that through reading this book with your children, you can help them and yourself cope with feelings of grief, doubt, anger, fear, and attain acceptance and peace through Jesus.

9 781644 580301